I Do Solemnly Declare

A play

Simon Farquhar

Samuel French—London
New York-Toronto-Hollywood

SET AVAILABLE

© 2001 BY SIMON FARQUHAR

Rights of Performance by Amateurs are controlled by Samuel French Ltd, 52 Fitzroy Street, London W1T 5JR, and they, or their authorized agents, issue licences to amateurs on payment of a fee. **It is an infringement of the Copyright to give any performance or public reading of the play before the fee has been paid and the licence issued.**

The Royalty Fee indicated below is subject to contract and subject to variation at the sole discretion of Samuel French Ltd.

>   Basic fee for each and every
>   performance by amateurs   Code D
>   in the British Isles

The publication of this play does not imply that it is necessarily available for performance by amateurs or professionals, either in the British Isles or Overseas. Amateurs and professionals considering a production are strongly advised in their own interests to apply to the appropriate agents for written consent before starting rehearsals or booking a theatre or hall.

ISBN 0 573 12282 2

Please see page iv for further copyright information

I DO SOLEMNLY DECLARE

First performed at Aberdeen Arts Centre as part of the Scottish Community Drama Association Festival of One-Act Plays on 24th February 1997. The cast was as follows:

Nigel Sheridan	Simon Farquhar
Eve Sheridan	Dianne Hogg
Gemma Sheridan	Jenny Tims
James Sheridan	Sandy Lamb

Produced and directed by Simon Farquhar
Stage Manager Oliver Knox

COPYRIGHT INFORMATION
(See also page ii)

This play is fully protected under the Copyright Laws of the British Commonwealth of Nations, the United States of America and all countries of the Berne and Universal Copyright Conventions.

All rights, including Stage, Motion Picture, Radio, Television, Public Reading, and Translation into Foreign Languages, are strictly reserved.

No part of this publication may lawfully be reproduced in ANY form or by any means — photocopying, typescript, recording (including video-recording), manuscript, electronic, mechanical, or otherwise — or be transmitted or stored in a retrieval system, without prior permission.

Licences are issued subject to the understanding that it shall be made clear in all advertising matter that the audience will witness an amateur performance; that the names of the authors of the plays shall be included on all announcements and on all programmes; and that the integrity of the authors' work will be preserved.

The Royalty Fee is subject to contract and subject to variation at the sole discretion of Samuel French Ltd.

In Theatres or Halls seating Four Hundred or more the fee will be subject to negotiation.

In Territories Overseas the fee quoted in this Acting Edition may not apply. A fee will be quoted on application to our local authorized agent, or if there is no such agent, on application to Samuel French Ltd, London.

VIDEO-RECORDING OF AMATEUR PRODUCTIONS

Please note that the copyright laws governing video-recording are extremely complex and that it should not be assumed that any play may be video-recorded for *whatever purpose* without first obtaining the permission of the appropriate agents. The fact that a play is published by Samuel French Ltd does not indicate that video rights are available or that Samuel French Ltd controls such rights.

CHARACTERS

Nigel Sheridan, late 30s
Eve Sheridan, his wife; late 30s
Gemma Sheridan, their daughter; mid-teens
James Sheridan, their son; mid-teens

The action of the play takes place in the living-room of the Sheridans' family home deep in suburbia

Time — the present

I DO SOLEMNLY DECLARE

The living-room of the Sheridan family home deep in suburbia. Early evening

There is a single door, R; this leads off to the kitchen, hallway and front door. The room is a little in need of redecoration as if the happiness of the family is taken for granted and not worked at. There is a sofa at an angle L, with a handbag on it; a table with a selection of drinks and glasses DL; and a long sideboard along the wall displaying the usual selection of ornaments, family photographs, a vase of flowers and some birthday cards. R is a small dining table, with chairs, and in front of this a television

It becomes clear that when the characters stare out to the audience they are looking through an imaginary window on to other homes in the sensible suburbs. The street never changes, there is no noise, no disorder, everything is safe

When the play begins, a brief chorus of "Suburbia" by The Pet Shop Boys rings out. The Lights come up to reveal James and Gemma seated on the R of the table, their mother Eve opposite them. Both children are in their mid-teens, and dressed very differently. Gemma is quite prim and reserved, James is more extrovert. Eve is in her late thirties. She is attractive and takes pride in her appearance, but is dressed and made-up to look motherly and respectable, with no hint of vanity. In her clothes and manner, as much as in her surroundings, she is old for her years. Each of the three is holding up a pair of playing cards; Eve has a drink in one hand too. All three figures are momentarily frozen; then James cautiously selects one of his mother's cards

During the opening exchange, Eve stares into space

James Damn. (*He throws down his cards in frustration and goes to sulk on the sofa*) I'm sick of this, you just bloody cheat the whole time.

Gemma Bloody hell, you're pathetic. Showing off just because you lose a stupid game of cards. (*With a teasing smile*) Child!

James Look, shut up, will you?

Pause

Gemma (*with mock tenderness*) Want to play something else?

James (*evenly*) No.

Gemma All right, all right, moody. (*She moves to the sideboard and produces a Scrabble set from it*) Scrabble? All right, Mum?

Eve downs the last of her drink and nods, trying to flash a smile

(*Setting the game up; to James*) Oh, for God's sake stop sulking. Spoilt brat.

James Get stuffed.

Gemma (*moving to James and pulling his ear*) I'm sorry, what was that?

James (*in agony*) OK, OK, I'm sorry.

Gemma And the rest.

James I'm sorry my darling sister for being so rude and so immature.

Gemma Come on, then.

James and Gemma smile and return to the table, the picture of happiness. James holds up a finger behind Gemma's back

James Dad's late. (*Pause*) Mum? Hallo?

Eve (*suddenly alert*) Mmm?

James I said Dad's late.

Gemma He was going to the TV studios this afternoon. He's probably got held up.

I Do Solemnly Declare

The game is now completely set up

   Right, I'm going first.
James Bloody hell.
Gemma Whose birthday is it?
James (*wearily*) Go on, then.

Gemma pauses, considers for a moment, then lays letters on the board

Gemma A-D-U-L-T. Adult. (*To James*) Maybe one day.
Nigel (*off*) I'm home.

Eve moves to pour another drink

   Nigel enters, carrying a leather briefcase and a small Harrods carrier bag. He is in his late thirties, flamboyant and wearing a respectable suit. He waltzes in full of energy and enthusiasm despite it being the end of a long day. His home seems to reflect his character very little, suggesting his thoughts are usually elsewhere

Eve does not even turn to look at her husband as he enters; she stands by the drinks table holding her refilled glass

Gemma \
James } (*together*) Hi Dad.
Nigel (*cheerfully*) Hallo! (*He presents the shopping bag to Gemma and kisses her*) Happy birthday, darling.

Gemma dives into the bag and produces a compact disc

   (*Ruffling James' hair*) Hiya, son. (*To Gemma*) That's just a little extra something I saw today. Is it the right one?
Gemma Yes thanks, it's great.

Nigel goes over to Eve and makes to kiss her on the cheek

Nigel Hi, darling.

Eve swiftly turns away and sits back down. Nigel stands still for a moment, looking a little puzzled but unconcerned

(*Reflecting quietly, comically*) What the hell have I done?
James What was the review like?
Nigel (*in an instant a master of ceremonies, amusing and entertaining to behold*) It seems, old son, that our national press, in all their wisdom, when they're not attached to the bottoms of the Royal Family, are as incapable as they ever were at producing an intelligible review of something. (*He opens his case and produces a copy of the* Evening Standard *which he reads from*) I quote: "Those who sat through the play "Unlawful Impediment" last night might well ask why an hour and a half was devoted to the age old theme of true love when nothing was said that we didn't already know." (*He breaks off*) The joys of omniscience … (*He returns to the paper*) "This curious tale of a man's affection for his girlfriend's mother was stretched to breaking point as the intricacies of each character's emotional turmoil were explored endlessly, all to little avail. Stark urban backgrounds were contrasted uneasily with the man's desperate attempt to combat social stigma in order to find happiness in a cruel modern world. An unpleasantly cynical sense of humour" — me? — "made an odd bedfellow with the notion that 'love hopes to conquer all in a world too strong for it.' An unsatisfactory ending claiming that 'all that is permitted in poetry is laughed at when tried out on society' fell flat on the ear. Perhaps love and love alone does justify ninety minutes and three painfully ordinary characters, but writer Nigel Sheridan must do more before I am convinced." I'd hate to be this guy's wife. "Mixing the sonnets of Shakespeare with the grime of urban reality made for a very bitter-sweet cocktail I for one found hard to swallow and left an unpleasant aftertaste." Thank you very much.
Gemma Never mind, you're always saying there's no such thing as bad publicity.
Nigel Yes I know.

James Did you go to the TV studios?
Nigel I did.
James What were they like?
Nigel Like bloody actors. I am never going to a read-through again. This clown with the incredibly sensible name of Stevie Stevenson decided that the line "You're a frump" was (*he does a "luvvie" impersonation*) "impossible for him to pull off convincingly." He wanted to rewrite it as "you're stupid." Er, I'm sorry Stevie, but the words "frump" and "stupid" are a little different in meaning. If I'd wanted to put "stupid" I would have put "stupid" and if I'd been thinking of you at the time I'd have been certain to. "Frump." A sixteenth century word meaning a dowdy, unattractive woman. "Tit." A twentieth century slang term for a stupid actor. (*He leans over Eve*) Sorry for swearing in front of the kids, dear.

No reaction

(*Surveying her again, then returning to his indulgences*) Whoever heard of actors rewriting their scripts? Actors aren't capable of doing important things like that. Show me one actor who could ever write a decent part for himself. They spend their lives quoting from plays they were never in and bitching about their colleagues who are working while they are "resting." They retire to sit in backstreet pubs and run sleazy second-hand bookshops where they explain that they retired because "the strains of playing the Dane became too much" and try to put other people off doing it because they're terrified they just might be a bit more successful. Bloody luvvies.

Gemma (*wearily*) Dad. Scrabble?
Nigel Definitely. (*He removes his jacket and puts it over the back of the sofa, then seats himself at the table*) I spent the rest of the afternoon devising the most amusing method of torturing Mr Stevenson. I think I eventually decided that two garlic presses, a cocktail stick and a pair of garden shears were essential to the purpose. Anyway that was my day. Do something for me, both of you: don't ever become actors. Otherwise I shall have to shoot you.

James I won't.

Nigel Excellent. (*To Eve, quieter*) Knocking those back a bit, aren't you? You OK?

Eve (*slowly turning to look Nigel in the eyes for the first time*) I'm fine.

Nigel Good. Whose go is it? And no silly modern words like "Netscape."

Gemma It's yours.

Nigel Oh, er — ah! (*He puts letters on the board*) S-H-A-P-E-R.

James Shaper? What's that?

Nigel A medieval shaman and storyteller, a man who fashioned the beliefs and fears of his people through his stories.

James (*tutting*) Your go, Mum.

There is a long pause

Eve (*putting letters on the board*) S-L-U-T. Slut.

Nigel (*unruffled*) Charming. Not talking about yourself, I assume.

James My go …

Eve (*putting more letters down*) And if you add E-R-Y to adult you get adultery.

Nigel (*after a pause*) Wow.

During the following, Eve rummages through the letters

Eve D-I ——

James Hey, hang on, Mum, it's my go.

Eve — V-O-R-C-E.

Nigel What are you doing?

Eve (*looking at the board*) D-I-V-O-R-C-E. Divorce.

Nigel (*comically bewildered*) You all right?

Eve M-I-S-T-R E-S-S spells mistress.

Nigel (*trying to make a joke of it*) Let's all play Happy Families.

Eve U-N-F-A-I ——

Gemma Mum, what's the matter?

Eve —T-H-F ——

I Do Solemnly Declare

Nigel (*to the children*) What's wrong with her?

Eve — U-L spells unfaithful. (*She hurls the board off the table*)

Nigel (*looking around for a moment, then at the children, then at Eve. Something in Eve's expression chills him*) Er ... Look, guys, why don't you run upstairs and have a listen to that CD.

James What's wrong with Mum? (*There is panic in his voice*) Dad? What is it?

Nigel I don't know but your mum's obviously not feeling herself and she's had too much to drink. Go on. Just give us a minute. Go on!

Gemma Mum?

Eve (*nodding slowly, with a faint smile*) Yes, go on. Just for a minute.

James and Gemma exit

Nigel (*calling after them*) We'll carry on in a minute. (*He springs over to Eve, his mood suddenly changing*) What the bloody hell are you playing at? What are you doing?

Eve B-A-S-T-A-R-D. Bastard. (*A crescendo*) Bastard. Bastard. Bastard.

Nigel Shut up! What the hell is the matter with you? What have I done? Well? You've just succeeded in wrecking our daughter's birthday because you're obviously four parts pissed, and what's all this about? (*He thrusts her head down to the board*) You think these are nice things for kids to see their mum spelling out in front of them, you stupid bitch? (*He lets go of her and looks in amazement at his hand, suddenly shocked by himself*) God, I'm sorry ... I'm sorry, I've never done something like that before ... I'm sorry, did I hurt you? (*He kisses her head, alarmingly concerned*) Come on, let's sit down. Tell me what's going through that silly little head. Come on ... Come on, I know you can feel bluesy when you've drunk too much.

Nigel tries to help Eve up but she won't budge

Come on, sit and talk to me.

He leads her over to the sofa. She moves like a zombie, her face expressionless. They sit together on the sofa. Nigel puts his arm round her and draws her head closer to him. Every move she makes is operated by him

   Now what's all this about, eh? Hey come on, this isn't like you. My beautiful, strong, brave Mrs. Sheridan.

Eve's face looks like it is about to melt into tears. Nigel hugs her but her arms are limp

   (*His voice becoming pained and worried*) God, what is it? Darling, please tell me. We always tell each other everything, don't we? Come on. What have you done today?

Eve I went shopping.
Nigel Uh-huh. And what did you buy?
Eve A new lamp for the bedroom.
Nigel Yes.
Eve And a few presents for Gemma.
Nigel Yes.
Eve And I ... I got you another bottle of that Norfolk Punch that you like.
Nigel Oh you didn't! (*He tries to make more of this*) Thank you. Look shall we have some? (*He gets up eagerly and heads for the kitchen, picking up his jacket*) Let's get this out of the way, yes?

Nigel exits

Eve (*staring ahead of her*) I was going to get a new dress.
Nigel (*off*) Well you should have done.
Eve (*shakily taking a cigarette from her handbag on the sofa and lighting it*) Harrods had some nice ones.

Nigel enters with a bottle of Norfolk Punch. He instantly freezes

Nigel Harrods?
Eve (*turning to him slowly, still seated*) Yes. Harrods.

I Do Solemnly Declare

Nigel When were you there?

Eve About two o'clock.

Nigel Oh, I was there getting Gemma's CD but that was ——

Eve I saw you.

Nigel No, I was there earlier.

Eve Who is she?

Nigel Who?

Eve The woman you were with.

Nigel What woman?

Eve The woman with the blonde hair. And the lovely smile.

Nigel I don't know what you mean. Darling, I've told you, I wasn't there at two.

Eve I saw you holding hands with her. And you kissed her by the entrance to Knightsbridge tube station.

Nigel But I ——

Eve I followed you. (*She pauses; the next words are a tense warning*) Don't lie to me.

Nigel (*slowly putting down the bottle and facing away from Eve*) It isn't what you think.

Eve No?

Nigel She's ——

Eve (*dreamily*) I couldn't believe it. I just looked up and there was my husband in the ladies' clothing section. Holding hands with another woman. Looking like love's young dream. How long has it been going on for?

Nigel (*kneeling beside her*) It's not like that. I met her a long time ago and I sometimes see ——

Eve I kept on thinking as I was coming home, what have I done wrong? Am I so inadequate? That he needs someone else. I've given him everything I have. I've given him two children so perfect it makes me cry. I keep his home clean and tidy. I cook him his dinner. I listen to what he has to tell me. I tell him everything. He's my best friend. And in an instant it's all gone.

Nigel Don't be silly. Of course it's not all gone. Listen ——

Eve It's all been a lie. I've been second best. Have there been others?

Nigel Of course not.

Eve Oh, that special is she?

Nigel It's not like that.

Eve Do you love her?

Nigel In a way.

Eve (*with hint of the bitterness to come*) And what way is that, darling?

Nigel (*walking away in frustration*) It's ——

Eve Do you love her?

Nigel I love you. There hasn't been a day we've been married that I've said that and not meant it.

Eve Do you love her?

Nigel Yes. (*He struggles with an impossible statement*) I love you too ——

Eve (*sarcastically*) — but in a different kind of way.

Nigel No. In exactly the same way. It is possible to love two people you know.

Eve (*slowly getting up and going over to him*) I ... I don't believe I'm hearing this. Am I supposed to feel thankful? That you do actually have feelings for me? I'm sorry. It's finished. Goodbye.

During the following Eve pours herself another drink, then stands examining the photographs on the sideboard, answering Nigel without looking at him

Nigel You can't just leave. Christ give us a chance to talk will you. All this has only been out in the open five minutes.

Eve I'm not leaving. You are.

Nigel What?

Eve I want you out of here.

Nigel This is our home. Jesus, just hang on will you, don't be so bloody silly ...

Eve Yes. And could you perhaps tell me when you decided that home wasn't good enough for you any more? When you decided that you needed more?

Nigel All right. All right, if you really want to know. (*He takes a cigarette*) When I woke up, my darling, to the fact that I wasn't dead yet. That I could have had a different life to this one. I was

I Do Solemnly Declare

trying to ... I don't know, I needed space. Look, when you're born, your life is open to anything, anything at all. (He *pours himself a scotch in a leisurely fashion*) Suddenly there I am at the altar — huh, aptly named place if ever there was one — and the whole of the rest of my life is decided for me from then on. To be tied to one place, one lifestyle, one role. One woman. And each day from then on life just went on like a needle stuck on a record. I wanted to make it as a writer. Did you encourage me? No. It was too *different* for you. Suddenly there I was in a new world, meeting new people who didn't have a care in the world, but always I had to be home by half-six for dinner. She ... When I met her she just ... She eclipsed you. I couldn't see you for her. It was one careless fling. I just let go, just once. OK, occasionally I still see her, but — it doesn't mean I don't want you.

Eve Really.

Nigel This is impossible. I — I couldn't live without you. And our children. I ——

Eve It's a bit late for that isn't it? I loved you so much I wanted to stay with you forever. I made the biggest commitment of my life to you. And you spat all that out on one extra-marital shag.

Nigel No. (*He reaches breaking point*) No, you wanted to stay with someone forever. I was just the one who was there, right place, right time. I fitted in as missing piece to fulfil your domestic dream.

The following exchange takes place at high speed; during the following, both characters sink to disorientated, desperate anger

Eve Oh, my poor dear, is all this so unbearable for you?

Nigel Yes.

Eve Were your fingers crossed when we slipped our wedding rings on?

Nigel No. No, I was certain then, and I'm certain now. I want you, God of course I do. I just want more. It's not sex, it's nothing to do with sex, it's about getting a life.

Eve (*calmer*) In that flat in Kensington when we were first married. You wrote poems about my face in the moonlight. And I thought,

"Is this guy ever going to stop telling me he loves me?" Well now I suppose you have.

Nigel No I haven't.

Eve And then moving into this place, those long weekends in Brighton, teaching James to ride his bike, pretending to them that Father Christmas was real.

Nigel Yes, when we started out it was all a big adventure. It made us feel oh-so-grown-up. But, Christ, we were eighteen. You had it all so worked out. Ambitions to do nothing for the rest of your life. Except go to coffee mornings with your friends, force feed me the *Daily Mail* gossip column, window-shop other lifestyles through that television and never dream of buying one of them. (*He gestures around the room*) All this, it's an alternative to living. It stopped being fun, Eve. That bloody suburban syndrome — it stopped being fun. You told me it was all so pie-in-the-sky, wanting to write. Well, now I'm there, and looking down my love, this looks pretty dismal ——

Eve *(together)* The lowest of the low can't look down.
Nigel You and all your friends, you'd never dare even venture out of the front door at night, would you?

Nigel Have you ever seen the world at three o'clock in the morning? Don't you ever want to? Breakfast, kids to school, shopping, home. (*He points at Eve's head*) Breakfast, kids to school, shopping, home. Breakfast, kids to school, shopping, home. A sauna in kitchen-sink drama.

Eve And you think you could live without all that, do you? I have a few simple things in my life. They're not much, but they're enough for me.

Nigel And that's what it means to be happy today, does it? Giving up on everything. Everyone shutting themselves into little coffins with just one slot for the newspaper to fall through every day, just to keep them in touch with what's outside. Stepping outside just to destroy yourself for a mortgage or to gather the food you need to keep alive? What for? Look. Look out there! What do you see? Company cars, Neighbourhood Watch stickers, leaves swept into neat rows on the pavements. Next year maybe a foreign holiday,

I Do Solemnly Declare

or a bigger car if I get that promotion. Laura Ashley curtains to impress the neighbours and to shut them out. That's all you've ever wanted. Playing "Covet Thy Neighbour's Life" but only for his big swimming pool and his freshly mown grass. I tell you what I see. I see dead bodies. The workers of our proud nation all drifting home with bags under their eyes as heavy as the ones under their arms. You know what they are? They're the five o'clock shadows. They're not real people any more. All of them in this — in this maze of Lily-white Gardens and Middle-Class Avenues, imprisoned each night in it like a giant concentration camp they can't leave because they don't think of it. Not settled down. (*He picks up a bottle and takes an ugly, greedy swig*) Becalmed.

Eve And that's what this is all about? (*Belittling Nigel*) You're a writer. You need to taste as many mouths as possible. Give yourself the experience so that one day you can tell your grandchildren how adored you were. Only you got it the wrong way round, didn't you? You got stuck with me at the start. (*Slowly*) It's enough for most normal people.

Nigel Well, I'm not most normal people.

Eve Have you forgotten already? Coffee and croissants in bed on a Sunday morning? Reading the colour supplement together? Snuggling up on the settee together watching late night television? Holding hands in the supermarket queue? It stopped being fun, did it? Domestic bliss? Well, that's what it was for me. Bliss. Me and my kind, keeping the home fires burning, we don't even have the opportunity to *think* about anything different. We have to be *strong*. You couldn't survive without us.

Nigel Oh, well, let's hear it for suburban suffragettes.

Eve Not suffrage. Suffering. We don't have time for any other interests. *This* is enough for me.

Nigel Well, that says a great deal about you, my dear. Perhaps if you'd shown some interest, some encouragement, maybe I wouldn't have had to look elsewhere. She was the first person who ever ——

Eve (*exploding*) I don't give a fuck about your stupid writing. But of course, it's all a higher good to you, isn't it? It's more important than a few people's happiness. I suppose she just adores it all, does she? All this isn't good enough for her. Why can't you just grow up? Trying to recapture your youth, it's so pathetic.

Nigel God why do you always have to think like that. It's such damned tunnel vision. It's so fucking apathetic. We never had any youth. I want to have done something with my life, tasted something different. Not just be locked into you until we're both too old to feel anything any more. (*He stops, feeling he has overreached himself*)

There is a silence. Eve slowly walks up to Nigel and begins playing teasingly with his tie. Suddenly she pulls the tie tight and Nigel begins to choke. Eve holds it tight, vengefully staring at him

Eve Do your family ties strangle you that much, my darling? Are we that much of a burden to you? (*She releases him*)

Nigel No. Not you. All this.

Eve Well, I'm afraid that's the way it has to be in this world, pet. Family trees aren't something you can just climb out of. You're stuck with us. If you really care for your loved ones you don't play stupid games.

Nigel Of course I care. I don't want us to end up like all them out there, playing it *safe*. That's what this is, a little safe. Stay shut inside a safe for too long and you can't move any more, you don't even have the will left to climb out of it. The light hurts your eyes.

Eve But what about me? (*Her tone changes to icy teasing. She is half temptress, half bitter wreck. She unbuttons her blouse slightly and perhaps lets her hair down. She stalks Nigel, cat-like, toying coolly with her drink*) That would be different, wouldn't it? You'd be *jealous. I* remember when we first met. You were so *jealous* if I even so much as commented on another man. You had this drive for me and you couldn't even bear my being touched by someone else. Maybe you only ever married me so that you could tie me down. You gave me two kids to act as padlocks, just to make sure I couldn't escape. And this other bitch. That's what you've done to her too isn't it? I bet she isn't allowed any other lovers. Well, let me tell you a little home truth, darling. I look at

I Do Solemnly Declare

other men. Yes! Unimaginative little me! I look at them at the traffic lights, in the street, on the television, in the supermarket. I look at them (*very spitefully*) and sometimes I *want* them. Oh, yes. I *want* them. I want to feel them all over me, I want to taste them, experience them — *have* them. Sometimes I flirt with them just for the thrill of it; a little revolution every so often. That's what I think sometimes when you're — out. Maybe wanting is as bad as doing. So don't think I'm going to play the little woman, ever faithful, who's been shut away all these years and depends on you. You always were *weak*. You think there's something strong in what you've done? Something manly? Well it's just the opposite. Only strong men make strong husbands. You've failed. (*She moves up close to Nigel. Hissing*) Bastard.

Nigel, looking as if he is on the verge of tears and very fragile, walks up to Eve, then suddenly grabs her. He is not so much aggressive as desperate

Nigel Spiteful bitch. Are you going to throw away everything we've got just for your own petty revenges?

Eve Me? Why Nigel? Why *her*? Why just *her* for all these years? (*Pause*) Come on. You might as well get it *all* out in the open. Why *her*? Fidelity doesn't appear to have been one of your strong points, so why always *her*? Good in bed, is she? Really (*she whispers*) turns you on, does she? Why? Why *her* for all these years, why?

Nigel (*wrenched from him finally*) Because we have a child.

There is a long pause. Eve stands paralyzed, in shock; Nigel is disorientated, shaking, amazed at his own admission. He cannot bear to look Eve in the eyes. He slowly moves to the sofa and collapses on to it. In the background, Eve walks unsteadily to the table and slumps down on to a chair

Eve Oh God no, please, God no. (*She leans her head on the table and sprawls her arms out*)

Nigel (*not looking behind him*) We have a little boy. He's seven.

Eve cries bitterly. Nigel immediately goes to her and strokes her hair, afraid to really touch her. He stands looking at her, like a murderer over a corpse

Gemma enters and stands in the doorway

Nigel turns to see Gemma. Gemma moves into the room, focusing intensely on her father as if possessed, with an expression of pure hatred. Nigel backs off in fear. Eve cries unbearably loudly, but this does not disturb Gemma. Without breaking her gaze she reaches down and rests a hand on her mother's shoulder. Eve starts and looks up. Gemma stands still, staring at Nigel

Gemma My brother is upstairs on his bed. Crying like a baby. Each one of his tears is the sweat from your passionate affair, *Daddy*. Huh. It's funny. It used to freak me out enough that you and mum must have sex sometimes.

Eve I'm sorry. I'm so sorry. I've ruined everything. It was supposed to be your birthday.

Gemma Yes, and what a birthday surprise eh, Daddy?

James enters. He is very fragile

James Gemma, leave it, will you? Mum and Dad need to talk this thing through.

Gemma Shut up. You're just the same as him. Just as weak. (*To Nigel*) Well, we don't need you.

James What are you saying? Don't be ridiculous.

Gemma (*eyes still boring into Nigel*) You're not wanted.

Eve slowly stands up and faces Nigel too

We want you to go.

Nigel sits back down

I Do Solemnly Declare

Did you not hear me?

Nigel (*quietly*) Don't talk to me like that.

Gemma Oh, sorry. Got to respect my elders and betters. Look at you. If your mistress could see you now. If all your *readers* could see you now. A pathetic, weak man. You've murdered my mother tonight twice over. And all of us.

Nigel Look. I understand how impossible all this is for you to take in. It's going to take a long time. But it doesn't affect the way I feel about you, God help me it doesn't.

Gemma Well, it changes the way we feel about you. Aren't we the little millstones round your neck, holding you back from your carefree lifestyle? Well, go on then. Walk away. (*Pause*) I said go.

Nigel You can't mean that.

Gemma Oh, yes, I do. For Mum's sake. Go off to your other family. You didn't do very well, did you? Your little pretence at escape got you tied down twice over, didn't it? Another failure. Since that's what you see all this as. A shrine to your failure. You're wrong though. It's your screwing it all up that's the failure.

James He didn't mean all that stuff, you know he didn't.

Gemma Well, it sounded bloody convincing to me.

Nigel You can't think I view you as callously as that. When I walked into that hospital ward and saw the woman I loved holding a new human being, one created out of our love, I'd never felt anything like it ever before. Nothing in the world can ever equal that feeling.

Gemma Sorry, was that when one of us was born, or the other one; it's hard to tell.

Nigel (*moving to Eve*) Look, if that moment still means anything to you then surely you're not going to destroy this family and just feed them the wreckage.

Gemma Oh, no. Don't you dare try and make Mum out to be the villain. I don't believe this. You think she owes you something? Don't you think we'd all be better off without you in our lives? We'd be better off with someone who was strong, with some sense of what it means to be a father. (*She looks at Eve*) And a husband. Not some weak overgrown child desperately trying to prove to himself that he's virile. I sometimes think about when I'll get married. When I do, my children will be my life. If I screw it up, I'll be scarring them forever. One little affair was that important to you, was it? You traded us in for that?

Nigel But don't you see, you *are* my life? One stupid mistake and I've had to go on paying for it. Did you really expect me to turn my back on another child of mine?

Gemma Oh, how *very* commendable. Did you get turned on by the danger of it? You kept on screwing her, didn't you? Just because she was there, was it? When you were with her, we didn't exist to you. Well, we don't exist the way you want us to any more. I don't know who I am any more. I don't know who you are any more. You're not my dad. You're just some stranger who walked in here tonight and destroyed this family. Why did you marry Mum? If you wanted other women, then why?

Nigel Gemma, when I stood at that altar I was totally sure. And I still am. Your mum — you're asking for yourselves not to have been born.

Gemma And why not? I might as well have not been born. You've destroyed all my past now, all my childhood memories. You've blackened every image, graffitied over every holiday snapshot we ever took. (*She snatches a photograph from the sideboard*) Remember that holiday, Daddy? Look at your face in that photo. The picture of happiness, aren't we? What was on your mind just then, eh? Were you counting the hours before you could see her again? Go to bed with her again? *Have* her again? Did you go round and screw her the minute we got back?

Nigel suddenly darts up, spins round and slaps Gemma

Nigel Shut up! (*He freezes, in shock*)

Gemma seems unaffected, her head turned away by the force but her expression unchanged. She eyes Nigel again

Oh my God I'm sorry. I'm so sorry... (*He makes to comfort her*)

Gemma sinisterly distances Nigel with an outstretched arm. Nigel retreats back to the sofa and sits, lifelessly

I Do Solemnly Declare 19

Gemma She's been a part of your life for all this time. You've never been all ours. Half of you was always with her. Damn you. You've junked all our pasts. My dad's dead now. Maybe the dad I loved, my hero, never really existed. To me it means fuck all now. (*She moves to the table*) This is not a birthday party, it's a wake. (*She picks up a glass and holds it up as if to make a toast*) Ladies and gentlemen, boys and girls, we are gathered here today to mourn the tragic, sudden death of the Sheridan family. Apparently the cause had been present for some time, but was undetected. Curiously it was the shock of the discovery that actually killed them. They will be sadly missed. (*She slowly puts the glass down, stares hard at Nigel, then walks away*)

Nigel gets up and heads for the exit. He pauses briefly and awkwardly by the other three, then exits

Eve (*unsteadily clearing the table*) Er ... let's ——
James Mum, what are you doing?
Eve Tidying up. The party's over isn't it?

After a pause of a few moments, Nigel enters with an overcoat and an overnight bag. He stands in the doorway

Gemma (*without turning round, her tone carrying a trace of uncertainty now*) As you can see I've packed an overnight bag for you. You can get the rest of your stuff tomorrow when we're at school.
Nigel Thank you. I'd best be ——
Gemma Don't forget your precious writing materials.

Nigel picks up his briefcase

James No. Dad, no. Look, come on everyone, we're all saying things we don't really mean because we're in shock. You're ... You're all my life, all of you. (*To Gemma*) You, are you going to throw all this away? Please! We'll all feel differently in time. We love our dad. (*He grabs Gemma by the shoulders*) Say it, "We love our dad."

Gemma is silent

"We love our dad." (*He grows more desperate*) "We love our dad!" Mum, you don't understand what this will do to us all. To me. I don't care if you don't love him. I don't care if you hate him. But please don't split up. I've got nothing left to believe in any more if the most important thing in my life breaks in two. (*To Nigel and Eve*) Look at each other. You belong standing next to each other. That's how you've always been to me. Like in all the photographs. Always smiling. Come on, (*he laughs feebly*) the camera never lies. You always smiled. You've been different people tonight. Just please, go back to the way it was. The way it was up until half an hour ago. The way it has to be. If we just pretend everything's all right then it will be. Mum, come on. Say it. "I love my husband." Say it, please! "I love my husband. I love my husband."

Nigel I'm sorry, son. I'll see you soon. (*He turns to leave*)
Eve I love my husband.
Nigel (*slowly turning round*) What?
Eve I love my husband. He is my life. I can't live without my husband. I want to forgive my husband. He is stupid and weak. But I can't imagine life without him.

Nigel puts down his bag and slowly moves to Eve, looking incredulous. She looks at him, a faint smile in her eyes

Nigel I'm sorry. I'm so sorry.
Eve (*playfully touching Nigel's face*) I do believe we've just had our first row.

Nigel takes Eve's hand as if they are on their first date

Nigel I'm so sorry.
Eve No. I don't want us to live on sorrow forever. We can't do this to our children. Or to each other. We need each other, don't we?
Nigel Come and sit down.
Eve (*entranced, distant*) Will you stop seeing her?

Nigel Yes.

Eve Do you promise?

Nigel Yes.

Gemma Mum, what are you doing? We don't need him.

Eve Yes, we do. I do. People like me and your dad, we've both wanted to break free of all this tonight. But we can't. He's accused me of being so conventional. Well, here I am being different. Doing something wild and crazy. I'm forgiving him. Look at him. He can't leave all this. He makes one fumbled attempt and then goes on paying for it for the next seven years. Look at us. A pathetic weak dreamer and a broken homemaker. (*She pauses, then picks up the newspaper review*) The truth hurts, you know. (*She tears up the review*) It's over. There are no heroes. Not round here. Not any more. There are no happy endings. Forget all this dreaming. All that imagination, it just makes you unhappy. That can't be good for you. Other people don't bother with all that. Be content with what you've got.

Nigel Why? Why can't ...

Eve Oh darling do you think you could ever be anything else but this? No. That's better. Now are you going to stop chasing rainbows?

Nigel (*sceptically*) Yes.

Eve (*gleefully*) And stop dreaming, and using your imagination?

Nigel Yes.

Eve Good. You've just become a normal husband at last.

Black-out

FURNITURE AND PROPERTY LIST

On stage: Old sofa. *On it*: handbag
Table. *On it*: selection of drinks and glasses
Long sideboard. *On it*: ornaments, family photographs, vase of flowers, birthday cards. *In it*: Scrabble set
Small dining table. *On it*: pack of cards, glasses for **Gemma**, **James** and **Eve**
Dining chairs

Off stage: Leather briefcase containing *Evening Standard* and small Harrods carrier bag containing CD (**Nigel**)
Bottle of Norfolk Punch (**Nigel**)
Overcoat, overnight bag (**Nigel**)

LIGHTING PLOT

Practical fittings required: nil
One interior. The same throughout

To open: Interior early evening light

Cue 1　**Eve**: " ... become a normal husband at last."　　(Page 21)
　　　　Black-out

EFFECTS PLOT

Cue 1   Opening of play; when ready   (Page 1)
         Suburbia (*Pet Shop Boys*)

A licence issued by Samuel French Ltd to perform this play does not include permission to use the Incidental music specified in this copy. Where the place of performance is already licensed by the PERFORMING RIGHT SOCIETY a return of the music used must be made to them. If the place of performance is not so licensed then application should be made to the Performing Right Society, 29 Berners Street, London W1.

A separate and additional licence from PHONOGRAPHIC PERFORMANCES LTD, 1 Upper James Street, London W1R 3HG is needed whenever commercial recordings are used.